THE SPOOKY HALLOWEEN ACTIVITY BOOK

JANE BULL

DK

Penguin Random House

For Charlotte, Billy, and James

SECOND EDITION
Produced for DK by XAB DESIGN

Design Jane Bull
Text Penelope York
Photography Andy Crawford
Senior Editor Dawn Sirett
US Senior Editor Shannon Beatty
Additional Design Work Holly Price, Roohi Rais
Jacket Design Helen Senior
Additional Jacket Design Work Dheeraj Arora
DTP Designers Dheeraj Singh, Vikram Singh
Jacket Coordinator Issy Walsh
Production Editor Dragana Puvacic
Production Controller Inderjit Bhullar
Managing Editor Penny Smith; **Managing Art Editor** Ivy Sengupta
Deputy Art Director Mabel Chan; **Publisher** Francesca Young
Publishing Director Sarah Larter

FIRST EDITION
Design Jane Bull
Text Penelope York
Photography Andy Crawford
Design Assistance Claire Penny
Jacket Designer Andrew Nash
Managing Editor Mary Ling
Managing Art Editor Rachael Foster
DTP Designer Almudena Díaz
Production Controller Orla Creegan

This American Edition, 2023
First American Edition published as *The Halloween Book*, 2000
Published in the United States by DK Publishing
1745 Broadway, 20th Floor, New York NY 10019

Copyright © 2000, 2023 Dorling Kindersley Limited
DK, a Division of Penguin Random House LLC
23 24 25 26 27 10 9 8 7 6 5 4 3 2 1
001-333585-Jul/2023

A catalog record for this book is available from the Library of Congress.
ISBN 978-0-7440-8044-5

DK books are available at special discounts when purchased in bulk
for sales promotions, premiums, fund-raising, or educational use.
For details, contact:
DK Publishing Special Markets,
1745 Broadway, 20th Floor, New York NY 10019
SpecialSales@dk.com

Printed and bound in China

For the curious
www.dk.com

MIX
Paper | Supporting
responsible forestry
FSC™ C018179

This book was made with Forest
Stewardship Council™ certified paper—
one small step in DK's commitment to
a sustainable future. For more information
go to www.dk.com/our-green-pledge

Filled with Halloween magic!

Adult Alert Symbols

Projects in this book may require adult
assistance or supervision. When you see
the warning symbol above, children should
take extra care and ask an adult for help.

Before you and your child start an
activity, consider any hazards together
and ways to avoid them. If your child
has long hair, make sure it is tied back
and out of the way.

Protect the area where children will be
carrying out the activities and encourage
them to wear old clothes or an apron.
Being prepared lets children enjoy
themselves to the fullest.

Trick-or-treat safety for children

- always go out with an adult
- only visit houses you know
- don't bother people who don't
  want to get into the spirit
  of Halloween
- ask an adult to check for allergens
  in party treats or treats you
  collect when trick-or-treating

WITHIN THIS SPOOKY BOOK YOU'LL FIND...

LIGHTS AND DECORATIONS

DRESSING UP

PARTY TIME

FLICKERING JACK-O'-LANTERNS

Keep away grumbling ghouls, sinister spirits, and ghastly ghosts on Halloween night by positioning your jack-o'-lanterns in a window. Dim the room lights, then light the candles, and watch the cackling faces flickering in the eerie darkness!

Scare away ghosts and demons with chilling, flickering faces in your windows.

Ask an adult to light the candles and to place them in the jack-o'-lanterns

HOW TO MAKE
FLICKERING JACK-O'-LANTERNS

Take the biggest, smoothest pumpkin you can find and carve a fantastic, jeering jack-o'-lantern. It will scare off ghostly Halloween creatures, keeping them far away from your house on the spookiest night of the year.

Spook to you soon!

Pen

Knife

Spoon

Bowl

Tea light candle

TURNIP HEAD

There are different vegetables you can use. Why not try slicing a turnip face? Turnips were used in Ireland, where the jack-o'-lantern originated. Watch out when you carve, however. Turnips are tough!

⚠ CANDLE MAGIC

Faces make very effective warnings, but simple patterns look great, too. Tea lights (small round candles) are the safest candles to use. Ask an adult to light the candle and place it in the pumpkin. Then pop the lid back on, and watch it twinkle in the darkness.

⚠ Ask an adult to help you cut the pumpkin, gouge out the inside, and carve the face.

1 Take a knife and chop off its head.

2 Gouge out the inside.

3 Draw a face.

4 Cut out its eyes.

SILHOUETTE WINDOWS

Swooping bats and petrified pumpkins silhouetted in your windows will startle any passer-by.

You can choose different colored tissue paper for different areas.

Cut out parts of your Halloween picture.

Draw your silhouette picture on paper. Black paper works well.

Ask an adult to help you cut out the picture with safety scissors.

Tape tissue paper to the back of the picture.

Overlap the two ends and tape them to make the lampshade shape.

⚠️ MAGIC LAMP

Why not spook up a lamp? Measure your lampshade, then use safety scissors to cut the lamp's shape out of black paper. Draw a Halloween picture on the paper and ask an adult to help you cut it out with safety scissors. Stick the paper onto your lamp, and turn the lamp on!

HAUNTED HOUSE

Use different tissue paper colors to create a colorful silhouette picture. A haunted house design is perfect for Halloween. You can make it look like the lights are on—but is anyone at home?

JEERING JARS

As dusk falls on Halloween, it's time to create some shadowy lights to decorate your yard or windowsill. You can jazz up a jar or transform a vase. And maybe some ghosts and spirits might be guided by your spooky lights!

Make your way at the witching hour in creepy candlelight!

Ask an adult to light the candles and to place them in the jars.

HOW TO MAKE JEERING JARS

Collect some glass jars or vases, any shape or size, and some bright tissue paper or plain tracing paper and you are ready to start making your jeering jars.

NIGHT JAR

One way you can decorate a jar is with some tracing paper. Either use a marker to draw a picture on the tracing paper, or cut out paper shapes with safety scissors and stick them on. Wrap the paper around the outside of the jar and light the candle.

Use safety scissors to cut black paper into shapes, and then stick them to the tracing paper.

Instead of sticking on Halloween paper shapes, you could draw a spooky picture on the tracing paper using a black marker.

• Ask an adult to light the candles and to place them in the jars. Tea lights (small round candles) are the safest candles to use.
• Make sure that you put the paper on the outside of the jars (not the inside).

⚠ TISSUE PAPER FACE

Tissue paper decoration works well on a jeering jar, and a face is a great image to use. The light shimmering through the face will drive off any wandering spirits!

Draw a face and ask an adult to help you cut it out with safety scissors.

Use safety scissors to cut some tissue paper to fit the jar.

Tape the tissue paper to the outside of the jar.

You could also add a layer of different colored tissue paper under the cut-out face.

Ask an adult to tie string securely around the rim of the jar. You'll also need adult help to light and place a candle in the jar, and hang the jar up.

Use safety scissors to cut tracing paper to fit around the torch with a 1/3 in (1 cm) overlap.

Next cut spooky shapes out of black paper with safety scissors and stick them on.

Tape down the join.

Wrap the paper around the end of the flashlight with the shapes on the inside.

Finally, use safety scissors to cut a frill out of crepe paper and stick it around the handle.

Turn it on and you're ready to go!

MAKE A FLASHY LIGHT!

Your friends will be green with envy when you shine your new flashlight. Go with an adult at dusk to see its full effect.

PAPER CHAINS

Screaming streamers are easy to make and a perfect decoration to hang around a table or on a wall. Be careful when you cut them—you don't want to separate your pumpkins or nose-to-nose cats!

Use safety scissors to cut out a long strip of paper, 4 in (10 cm) wide and however long you want. Fold the paper backward and forward to create square shapes and a concertina effect.

Folded edge →

Folded edges

Folded edges →

Folded edge

Draw a ghost on the folded strip of paper, making sure the drawing reaches each folded edge.

Cut out the ghost with safety scissors, leaving a part of the folded edges on each side uncut, so that the ghosts are holding hands when you unfold the paper.

Unfold the paper, decorate it, and hang it up! Pumpkin or cat designs work well, too.

COOL COSTUMES

Dressing up is one of the most exciting things about Halloween. Search your home, use a little imagination, get creative, and presto—you've got a prize-winning costume!

FACE VALUE

Decorating your face with face paint or wearing a mask can make all the difference to your costume. Turn to pages 20–27 to find out how to add face decoration to your Halloween look.

For the ghost's face, ask an adult to help you sew felt features onto a white sheet. Make holes in the eyes so that you can see through them.

Turn yourself as white as a sheet!

Be a groaning, grumbling ghost!

Say hocus-pocus to cast a spell!

A black T-shirt, black leggings, and some black gloves are a perfect, simple base for a cat costume.

Ask an adult to help you sew some black, pointy ears onto a headband.

A feather boa makes a great cat's tail or fur.

A witch's hat and nails can be bought from a local store.

Become a witch's cat. Meow!

A large piece of dark material draped around your head and shoulders makes a good cloak for a zombie costume.

Spooky gloves can be bought from a local store or created from rubber gloves.

HOW TO CREATE COOL COSTUMES

You don't have to spend a lot of time or money making a Halloween outfit. Simple costumes can be very effective. Here are some great ideas for creating cool outfits. Search around your house for objects you can use. Why not turn yourself into a pumpkin fairy or a pillaging pirate!

! • Follow the instructions that come with your face paint, and test for skin allergies before applying them.

Face paint and a sword are all you need for a pirate outfit. You could make a sword from cardboard.

Make a fairy tiara by decorating a headband.

Adapt a fairy outfit to create an orange pumpkin fairy.

Paint flowers and tendrils on your face with face paint.

Design an outfit with whatever you can find!

Collect clothes, toys, and pieces of material that you can use to make a costume.

Make a matching treat bucket (see pages 28–31).

You could attach ribbons to your shoes that match your fairy outfit.

A pumpkin mask and matching treat bucket make a fun costume. See pages 24–27 and 28–31 to find out how to make masks and treat buckets.

Make a witch hat out of thin black cardstock.

Make shirt cuffs out of thin cardstock and use gummies as cufflinks!

A large piece of material draped over your shoulders makes a good vampire cape.

A black dress and striped tights are perfect for a witch.

Find a scarf to tie around your head as a pirate bandana.

Remember to put on your shoes before you go from house to house!

Decorate a pirate hat with a skull and crossbones. Use safety scissors to cut a skull and crossbones from paper and stick it to the hat.

Be a little monster with a monster mask. See pages 24–27 to find out how to make masks.

Rolled-up, loose pants and long socks work well for a pirate outfit.

You can make skeleton gloves from rubber gloves.

For a skeleton outfit, use safety scissors to cut bones from paper. Stick them onto a black T-shirt. Then put on a spooky skeleton mask! See page 24 to find out how to make the mask.

Tie a scarf around your waist as a belt for the loose pants. You can also use it as a holding place for your cardboard sword.

FEARSOME FEATURES

It's amazing how a touch of face paint can change you into a fully fanged vampire or a grinning witch's cat. Choose a Halloween theme, paint your features, and challenge anyone to recognize you!

Shiver me timbers, give the pirate a treat!

⚠ Follow the instructions that come with your face paint, and test for skin allergies before applying them.

HOW TO PAINT FEARSOME FEATURES

Face paint is easy to use, but you have to take your time applying it to get the best results. Try practicing some face paint styles on paper. Then persuade your friends to let you create different looks on their faces! Remember that face paint can be messy, so have some towels handy.

Sponge for blending colors or covering large areas

Biodegradable glitter makeup for extra highlights

Eyeliner for fine details

Paintbrush for painting details

Water-based face paint

You can create more colors with your face paint by mixing colors together.

Follow the instructions that come with your face paint and hair gel, and test for skin allergies before applying them.

WITCH

1 Mix a pale purple face paint for the eyeshadow.

2 Use a sponge to dab the same purple onto your cheeks as blush.

3 Paint on black eyebrows and use eyeliner around your eyes.

4 Mix black face paint with the purple for the lipstick.

5 Add a creepy-crawly or two if you like!

BLACK CAT

1 Color around the eyes using white face paint.

2 Use a sponge to dab white face paint around the mouth and chin.

3 Paint the end of the nose and bottom lip with pink face paint.

4 Color black around the white painted part of the eyes.

5 Use black face paint around the mouth and all over the rest of the face.

6 Finish the face with some strokes of biodegradable glitter makeup.

PIRATE

1 Use black face paint to paint an eye patch over one eye. Add a painted strap.

2 Paint a big, hairy eyebrow over the other eye.

3 Use red face paint to paint some scars. Highlight them with white face paint.

4 Use a coarse sponge to dab on black stubble.

5 Scrunch up your face to help you position some black wrinkle lines.

SKULL

1 Wear a black hairband to frame the face.

2 Sponge on white face paint as a base color.

3 Paint big, black eye sockets.

4 Blend in yellow face paint to add to the bony look.

5 Draw some black cracks around the face. Color the lower cheeks black.

6 Create a creepy mouth with thin, black, vertical lines.

7 Color the nose in black face paint.

VAMPIRE

1 Slick back the hair using lots of hair gel.

2 Dab on white face paint with a sponge.

3 Rub some gray around the eyes to add to the vampire look.

4 Paint a hairline and eyebrows with black face paint.

5 Use a sponge to dab gray face paint along the cheekbones to narrow the face.

6 Paint gray below the eye sockets and add some red lines.

7 Color the lips gray and paint white fangs outlined in black and dripping with red blood!

SCALY MONSTER

1 Start by sponging yellow face paint over the nose and in the center of the face.

2 Use a sponge to dab green around the yellow and spread it over the face and hair.

3 Use red face paint for the eyeshadow and nostrils.

4 Use black face paint for the scales and lips, and also for the outlines around the eyes.

5 Paint on white fangs and outline them in black.

PAPER PLATE FACES

Send chills down the spines of your neighbors when you go out trick-or-treating by wearing these masks made out of paper plates. Try a creepy cat, a petrified pumpkin, a wicked witch, or a sinister skull!

Make a menacing mask from a plain paper plate.

⚠️ Ask an adult to help you cut through the plate, staple the slits, and attach the elastic.

1 Draw a face and cut it out with safety scissors.

2 Staple in the slits to shape the mask.

You can cut slits in the top, then staple, so the mask fits better.

3 Attach some elastic.

DECORATING PAPER PLATE FACES

Quick to make and fun to wear, these paper plate masks can be worn plain or decorated. Different colored paints bring the monsters and pumpkins to life!

Acrylic paint

Paintbrush

PVA glue

Transform yourself into a paper plate character!

⚠️ Ask an adult to help you with the cutting and stapling for each mask.

Use the whole plate for the pumpkin head.

Use part of the plate for the black cat. Cut around the mask with safety scissors.

The monster mask can be shaped by cutting slits in the chin and stapling in.

PUMPKIN HEAD

BLACK CAT

SPOTTED MONSTER

You could paint swirly green paint around the edge of the orange pumpkin, and also use green on the stalk and to outline the eyes, nose, and mouth.

Decorate the cat with different paint colors. Add some whiskers and a nose, and highlight the eyes and ears.

This blue monster mask has orange highlights and green spots. But you can use any colors and decoration on your monster mask.

1

Draw on your witch's features.

Mark on triangular slits at the top and bottom of the plate that you can cut out to shape the mask.

2

Ask an adult to help you use safety scissors to cut the facial features.

Cut the triangular slits at the top and bottom of the plate. Ask an adult to help you staple them in. This shapes the mask so it fits your face.

3

Paint the mask one color and highlight the mouth and eyes in another color. Add some warty dots..

4

WICKED WITCH

The crepe hair is a great addition to the warty witch mask. For a thicker head of hair, add more crepe tendrils to the mask.

Add green hair by using safety scissors to cut a sheet of crepe paper into strips. Tape the finished hair to the back of the mask.

BUCKETS OF TREATS

At twilight, when you and your grown-up go knocking on neighbors' doors, take one of these fun treat buckets to carry your candy. And why not make some cool paper cones, too. Fill them with treats for trick-or-treaters who knock on your door!

HOW TO MAKE TREAT BUCKETS

PUMPKIN PAIL

Create this pumpkin treat bucket to take with you when you and your grown-up go out and about. Remember to start making it before Halloween to let it dry in time.

Rub petroleum jelly on a balloon so that the balloon doesn't stick to the paper at the end.

Paste at least five layers of newspaper over the balloon.

Use wallpaper paste or a flour and water mix made with half a cup of flour and half a cup of warm water.

Create a bowl shape with the paper, and leave it to dry for two days. Rest the balloon on a wide glass or cup.

When the paper is dry, pop the balloon.

When the rim is dry, paint the whole bucket a single color.

Paste the rim of the bucket and stick on extra strips of newspaper folded over the rim.

When the base color is dry, paint a face on the side of the bucket in a different color.

A perfect pail for your tasty treats!

Ask an adult to make a hole in each side of the bucket. Thread a length of rope through the holes to make a handle.

LEAF OR STAR BUCKET

A quick way to make a Halloween treat bucket is to simply cover a plastic bucket with crepe paper. You could decorate the handle with pipe cleaner flowers, or use stickers for decoration.

Stand the bucket in the middle of the crepe paper. Fold the crepe paper over the rim of the bucket and secure it with tape.

Wrap a long strip of crepe paper around the handle, and secure each end with tape.

You'll need a good sized bucket with a handle, and a large sheet of crepe paper.

Use safety scissors to cut leaves or stars out of paper.

Tie the pipe cleaners to the bucket handle.

HALLOWEEN STICKERS

Draw Halloween pictures on blank sticky labels.

Color the pictures and then stick the stickers to your treat bucket or candy cones.

Tape the paper leaves or stars to the pipe cleaners.

Wrap each pipe cleaner around a pencil to create a swirly stalk effect.

CANDY CONES

These candy cones are perfect treats to give to those who turn up at your door wanting goodies. They are also ideal gifts to give to guests at the end of a Halloween party.

Fold one corner across the center, as shown.

Fold up the base and glue it down.

Take a sheet of paper, about 8 in (20 cm) square.

Fold the other corner over, as shown, and fix it down using a glue stick.

Decorate your candy cone with stickers.

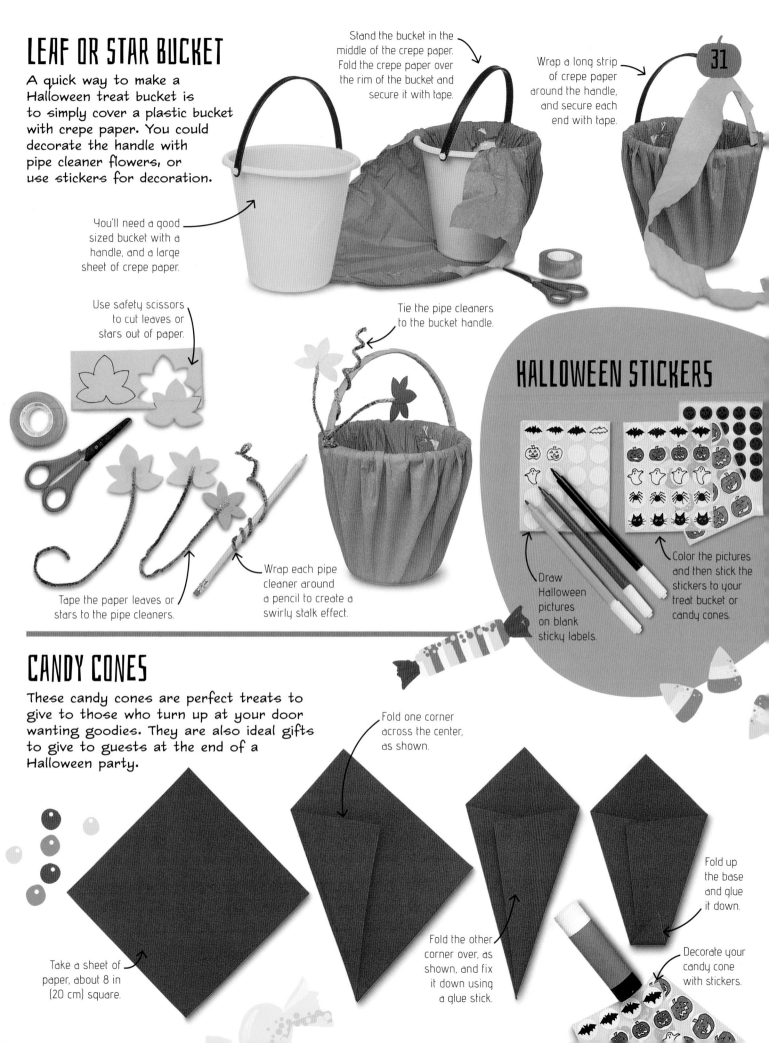

BEASTLY BUFFET

You can't have any old food at a Halloween party. You need a hair-raising banquet to serve to your ravenous guests. Make sure your table is groaning with gruesome goodies and some really horrifying snacks!

Ghostly cookies (see pages 38-39)

Savory bites
(see pages 34-35)

Creepy cupcakes
(see pages 36-37)

• Ask an adult to help you with the toothpicks. Remember to remove them before you eat the snacks.
• You may need adult help when you cut the vegetables and the shaped pizzas.
• Ask an adult to help you cook the pizzas.

SAVORY BITES

Make your guests howl with delight by serving them these sandwich monsters and pizza faces! Use vegetables such as peppers and olives to create fun faces that taste fantastic, too!

Here's a monster mouthful!

Use toothpicks to keep the bread features in place.

Create a soulful look with down-turned cucumber and olive eyes.

Ask an adult to help you cut a carrot into funny ear shapes.

These rolls are perfect for hungry party-goers.

A piece of salami makes a great floppy tongue.

MEGA MONSTERS

There are many different monsters you can make with sandwich rolls. Why not hold a contest with your friends to see who can make the most unappetizing creature for your beastly banquet!

Long green chives work well as creepy, spindly legs.

A row of corn kernels make goofy monster gnashers.

Ask an adult to help you cut a radish in half for some garish red eyes.

Ask an adult to help you cut the pizza base to make shaped pizzas.

Make sure you use your favorite pizza toppings. You want to enjoy your beastly bites!

FREAKY FACE PIZZAS

Ghostly faces on pizza bases make ghoulish party snacks. Why not challenge your friends to make their own pizza face?

Devour my gruesome hot dog fingers!

The tomato nails look like sharp talons on the ends of the fingers.

FINGER FEAST

Yuck! Dare your friends to chew on these gruesome nibbles! Make the fingers with cooked hot dogs, and add pieces of tomato or red pepper as fingernails. Pierce the fingers with toothpicks and ask an adult to help you poke them into an acorn squash or watermelon.

A ketchup-flavored dip works well with your finger buffet.

⚠ Be careful when using the toothpicks.

CREEPY CUPCAKES

Desserts normally look so inviting—not these creepy cupcakes though! Who would want to eat a big spider or a bulging eyeball? But if your guests dare to try these terrifying tidbits, they'll discover how tasty they really are!

Tubes of writing icing are perfect for creating fine, delicate patterns.

⚠ CUPCAKES

(makes 24 cupcakes)

$^1/_2$ cup softened butter
$^2/_3$ cup granulated sugar
1 cup flour
1 $^1/_2$ tsp baking powder
$^1/_2$ tsp salt
2 large eggs
1 tsp vanilla extract

Put the ingredients into a bowl and beat with an electric hand mixer until the mixture is creamy, about 2 minutes.

Divide the mixture equally between the 24 cupcake baking cups.

Ask an adult to help you bake the cupcakes for 18–20 minutes at 375°F (190°C).

WHITE ICING

2 $^3/_4$ cups confectioners' sugar
2 tbsp water
1 tbsp lemon juice

Add the water and juice to the confectioners' sugar and mix until smooth.

Use icing to make the legs of a gummy spider.

WOBBLY WEBS

These spiderweb cupcakes look great on a Halloween table. Will you be tempted to eat one?

Frost the top of the cake with white icing.

Draw a swirl with a tube of writing icing.

Use a toothpick to drag lines from the center of the swirl out to the edge. Be careful with the sharp ends of the toothpick. Add a gummy spider or one made from licorice to the web.

Different shaped candies are great for cake decoration.

RED EYE CAKES

The eyeball decoration is made with a maraschino cherry and black writing icing. Use red food coloring or writing icing for the veins.

Look into my eyes. What can you see?

⚠ Be careful when using food coloring because it can stain.

SPIDERS AND BUTTERFLIES

Gummy candies work well as wobbly insect bodies, and licorice rope makes good spindly spider legs. You can try your own insect cake designs with any candy you like.

GHOSTLY COOKIES

The great thing about this cookie dough is that you can cut it into any shapes you choose. If you want to hang up your cookies as decorations, make a hole in them to slip thread through when they are baked. But don't expect them to be hanging un-nibbled for long!

This is the actual size that the cookies can be, so you could trace around this ghost as a guide.

⚠ COOKIE DOUGH

(makes 12–14 cookies)

2 cups flour
11 tbsp butter
$^3/_4$ cup confectioners' sugar
Zest of half a lemon
1 tbsp milk

Put the flour, confectioners' sugar, and butter into a bowl. Rub these ingredients together with your fingers until they resemble crumbs. Add the milk and the lemon zest to the crumbly mixture, then knead it together to make a dough.

Chill the dough for 20 minutes. Then roll it out and cut your cookie shapes as shown.

Ask an adult to help you bake the cookies for 15 minutes at 325°F (160°C).

When the cookies are baked and cooled, add decorations, such as ghostly faces. Use a tube of writing icing to create the decoration.

Draw ghosts and other Halloween pictures on cardboard and use safety scissors to cut them out.

Roll the cookie dough until it's about $^1/_3$ in (1 cm) thick. Place your cardboard pictures on the dough.

Then use a knife to cut around your cardboard pictures to make beastly cookie dough shapes.

Put the cookies on a buttered baking sheet.

Ask an adult to help you pierce a hole in the top of each cookie with a toothpick. Be careful with the sharp ends of the toothpick.

Swinging ghosts make tasty tidbits!

HANGING UP

When the ghostly cookies are ready, simply slip some thread through their holes and ask an adult to help you hang them up. They'll look spooky hanging from branches in your yard. Or hang them from some string across a wall inside your home.

CAULDRON COCKTAILS

Drinks to leave you shaken and stirred are essential for every Halloween party. Entertain your friends with slimy, frothing, or vampire-blood colored drinks that look good and taste great.

Use paper or reusable straws—they are better for the environment.

Guzzle! Guzzle!

FREAKY FRUITY PUNCH

Mix this delicious drink that's perfect as a fruit punch, and serve it up in a pumpkin punch bowl. It will serve 10 very thirsty party-goers.

⚠ PREPARING THE PUNCH

35 fl oz (1 liter) apple juice
35 fl oz (1 liter) ginger ale
Fruit such as sliced apple, tangerine segments, sliced kiwi, and sliced grapes

Ask an adult to help you slice the fruit. Mix together the apple juice and ginger ale. Add the sliced fruit. You could cut the sliced apple or kiwi into star shapes using a star-shaped cookie cutter.

Serve your punch with a ladle.

Carefully place a bowl into your pumpkin cauldron and fill it with your punch.

PUNCH BOWL CAULDRON

What better way to serve your Halloween punch than inside a punch bowl cauldron made from a pumpkin? Ask an adult to help you hollow out and carve the pumpkin—see the instructions on page 7, which explain how to do this. Then mix some Freaky Fruity Punch or your own punch recipe, carefully place a bowl in the pumpkin, and pour in the punch.

I dare you to take a drink from my cauldron!

SPOOKY POTIONS

These hair-raising potions can be made by the glass as shown or in large quantities for your pumpkin-head cauldron. You may need the ice techniques below.

COLORED ICE

Be careful when using food coloring because it can stain.

Pour colored fruit juice or water mixed with a few drops of food coloring into an ice tray, and pop it into the freezer overnight—simple but effective!

CRUSHED ICE

To make crushed ice, put some clear or colored ice cubes into a bag, seal the top, and hit the ice hard with a rolling pin!

HOT CHOCOLATE BONES

Make this welcoming brew to warm the bones of the trick-or-treaters on their return.

1 tsp of cocoa powder
1 mug of hot milk
Some sugar to taste
Marshmallows

Ask an adult to help you heat the milk. Mix the cocoa powder with a small amount of the hot milk to make a paste. Pour in the rest of the hot milk and stir it. Add sugar to taste, and then the marshmallows—delicious!

LEMON AND LIME SLIME

Watch the amazement on your friends' faces when this drink goes green as the ice melts!

1 glass of lemon-lime soda
About 5 large green ice cubes (made with water and green food coloring)
1 slice of lime

Simply add the green ice cubes and slice of lime to the glass of lemon-lime soda.

Slurping the slime.

You could hang a toy creepy-crawly from the side of the glass.

Brewing the bones.

Decorate a spoon or straw with a paper skull. Use paper or reusable straws—they are better for the environment.

This drink turns green as the green ice melts.

Be careful with the sharp ends of toothpicks.

CANDY CORN CRUSH

Try sucking up this multicolored slushie through a straw. Or you can eat it with a spoon.

Crushed ice—use layers of crushed ice made from orange juice, cranberry juice, and water

The layers of this drink look like candy corn. Use the water ice at the bottom, then the cranberry juice ice, and finally the orange juice ice at the top.

VAMPIRE BROTH

Mix this broth in front of your friends and watch it come alive before your eyes!

1 glass of cola
1 scoop of vanilla ice cream

Fill the glass so that it's about two-thirds full with cola. Add a scoop of ice cream and STAND BACK!

WITCHES' BREW

Eye of newt, blood of bat, frog's tongue, and a squeeze of lemon—this is a brew with more than a few surprises!

$\frac{1}{2}$ cup cranberry juice
$\frac{1}{2}$ cup lemonade
A few drops of lemon juice
A few large green ice cubes (made with water and green food coloring)
1 gummy worm or snake

Mix the cranberry juice and lemonade together in a glass. Add the lemon juice, the green ice cubes, and then drape the gummy worm or snake over the rim of the glass.

Fixing the froth.

Combining the crush.

Mixing the magic.

Make your own paper candy corn and stick it onto a spoon.

Add a gummy worm or snake, slithering over the rim of the glass.

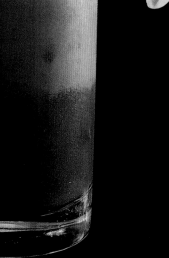

⚠️ Be careful that the froth doesn't fall on your clothes, floor, or furniture.

FUN AND GAMES

Games are an essential part of a really good Halloween party, especially if you provide prizes for the winners! With these creepy games, you'd better give a prize to anyone who is willing to play them—to reward their bravery!

If you cut off one side of the box, then you can watch and check that the person really does put their hand in!

It's slimy, eww!

⚠️ FUNNY FEELINGS

Only the bravest of guests should try this game! The idea is for each person to plunge their hands into nasty things that they can't see. YUCK! Ask an adult to help you use safety scissors to cut a hole in a box big enough to fit a hand through. Place a bowl inside containing something yucky.

Try some wet cooked spaghetti that will feel like worms or a peeled grape that might feel like an eyeball!

Be aware that this game causes lots of shrieks!

It's like going on a jittery journey!

GHOST TRAIN EFFECTS

All aboard the ghost express! Take your friends on a pretend trip to trembling towers. Sit one person on a chair and blindfold them. Use sound effects while moving things across their face. Cold ice will give a shock. And is that a hairy spider or just a feather?

Use your imagination and each player will use theirs.

⚠️ SHADOW THEATER

Do you know any really chilling ghost stories that will scare the living daylights out of your friends? If so, then here's a way to bring them to life. Ask an adult to help you hang a white sheet across a doorway. Then shine a bright light from behind you through the sheet.

Guaranteed to give your guests the goose bumps!

Tell your story from behind the sheet and you will appear as a spooky, shadowy figure. You could make cardboard props to help bring your story to life. Draw the props on cardboard and use safety scissors to cut them out.

One dark and moonlit night...

A large pair of freaky cardboard scissors or a spooky fish skeleton will impress your friends, or cut out any other cardboard props you need to help tell your story. Make plenty of creepy sounds to get everyone into the right mood.

PLUNGE IN GUNGE

Mix together some horrible gunge in a bucket. You could use a mixture of flour and water. Make the mixture thick. The idea is that you can't see through the gunge.

Place objects in the gunge such as washable toys, buttons, or pebbles, and dare your friends to plunge their hands into it to retrieve them.

A prize for anyone brave enough to delve into the unknown!

DANGLING DOUGHNUTS

Tie string around some doughnuts, as shown, and ask an adult to hang the doughnuts from a pole in a row. Tie each person's hands behind their back, line everyone up to a doughnut, and ask each player to MUNCH! The first person to finish their doughnut is the winner. You'll find that faces can become very sticky!

One extra rule—no lip licking!

TREATS AND DARES

A game of risk is always exciting to play. Use safety scissors to cut lots of small paper rectangles. Write dares on half the papers and treats on the other half. Pop the papers into a hat and ask your friends to pick at their peril! Dares could include standing on your head or doing a silly dance!

Treats could be candy or a small present.

You could decorate the back of your papers with stickers. Find ideas for turning plain stickers into Halloween stickers on page 31.

APPLE BOBBING

Fill a large bowl with water and drop some apples into it. You will find that they float. Ask each person to hold their hands behind their back while they try to retrieve an apple from the bowl using only their mouth. Anyone cheating is instantly disqualified, and WATCH OUT—the floor can get pretty wet!

Dunk! Splash! Crunch!

⚠ PUMPKIN SEEDS APLENTY

When you carve out your jack-o'-lanterns, you will find that you are left with lots of pumpkin seeds. You don't have to throw these seeds away. They are delicious to eat when roasted or they can be threaded onto string as Halloween decorations or jewelry.

Ask an adult to help you carve the pumpkin. See page 7.

⚠ ROASTED PUMPKIN SEEDS

2 cups pumpkin seeds
2 tbsp olive oil
1 tsp salt

Ask an adult to help you use the needle.

To roast your pumpkin seeds and turn them into a tasty snack, first rinse them in water. Then wrap the seeds in a clean dish towel and pat them thoroughly dry. Next mix the seeds with the olive oil and salt in a large bowl. Then spread them out on a baking sheet, and ask an adult to help you roast them for 12–15 minutes at 350°F (180°C).

To make jewelry or decorations, thread dried, rinsed seeds onto string.

Tie a knot in one end of the string before threading the seeds. Knot the string again when you finish.

TRICK-OR-TREATING SECRETS OF SUCCESS

● don't forget to take a treat bucket or bag, so you can carry all the goodies you collect!

● hint to your neighbors that you will be coming by—then you are likely to be offered more candy!

● check for food allergens in party treats or treats you collect when trick-or-treating

● be kind to your friends and share the Halloween candy you collect

INDEX

ACKNOWLEDGMENTS

DK would like to thank:
Emma Patmore for food styling;
Stephanie Spyrakis for face painting;
Charlotte Bull, Billy Bull, James Bull, Tex Jones, Kiana Smith, Kristian Revelle, Maisie Armah, and Elicia Edwards for being spooky models

DK would also like to thank the following for additional photography: Dave King for the Turnip Head on page 7, Gary Ombler for the witch on page 19, and Steve Shott for the witch on pages 19, 33, and 46